OXFORD

WILD READS

Rats

Jan Mark

OXFORD

UNIVERSITY PRESS

OXFORD
UNIVERSITY PRESS

Great Clarendon Street, Oxford OX2 6DP
Oxford University Press is a department of the University of Oxford.
It furthers the University's objective of excellence in research, scholarship,
and education by publishing worldwide in

Oxford   New York

Auckland   Cape Town   Dar es Salaam   Hong Kong   Karachi
Kuala Lumpur   Madrid   Melbourne   Mexico City   Nairobi
New Delhi   Shanghai   Taipei   Toronto

With offices in

Argentina   Austria   Brazil   Chile   Czech Republic   France   Greece
Guatemala   Hungary   Italy   Japan   Poland   Portugal   Singapore
South Korea   Switzerland   Thailand   Turkey   Ukraine   Vietnam

Oxford is a registered trade mark of Oxford University Press
in the UK and in certain other countries

Text © Jan Mark
Illustrations © Una Fricker
The moral rights of the author have been asserted

Database right Oxford University Press (maker)

This edition 2009

British Library Cataloguing in Publication Data

Data available

ISBN: 978-0-19-911930-1

1 3 5 7 9 10 8 6 4 2

Printed in China
Paper used in the production of this book is a natural,
recyclable product made from wood grown in sustainable forests.
The manufacturing process conforms to the environmental
regulations of the country of origin.

Contents

▶ True or false?

People say unkind things about rats.

Rats steal food.

Rats are dirty. They carry diseases.
They live in sewers.

Rats are savage. They have huge teeth. They jump up at people and bite their throats.

Rats have long, bald, horrible, scaly tails.

Most of these things are not true.

▶ Dirty rats

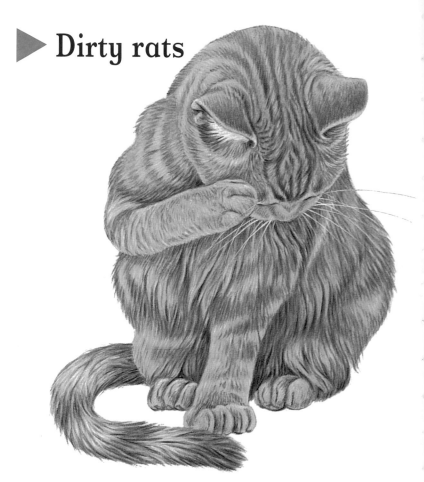

Watch a cat washing itself. It licks its paw and rubs the paw over its head and ears.

Did you know...
Rats do not have fur on their paws. In fact, their back paws look rather like human feet and their front paws are like hands.

A rat does the same thing, but a rat uses both paws at once.

Cats comb their fur with their teeth. So do rats. Cats scratch themselves with their back feet. So do rats.

Did you know...
Rats can hold things in their "hands", but they cannot use them the way we do. They have no thumbs. The only other animals that have thumbs are primates.

rat

primate

Cats hate to be dirty, and so do rats. They keep themselves very clean.

But they live in sewers, don't they?

Well, some rats do.

brown rat

Black and brown

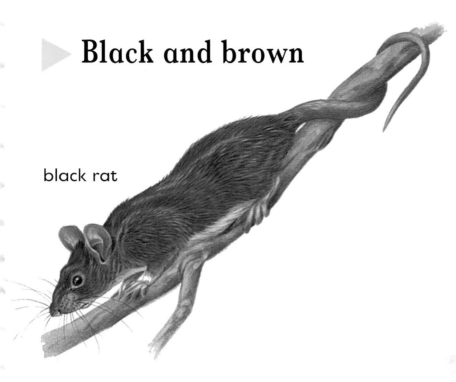

black rat

Different kinds of rats live in different kinds of places. There are many more brown rats than black rats in Britain, but the black rats were here first.

Black rats like to be high and dry. They used to live in trees. If they get into buildings they prefer to live upstairs.

Brown rats make burrows and want to be near water. They live on river banks if they can. They are good swimmers. In buildings they try to live underground in cellars, where it is damp.

Did you know...

The brown rat is called the Norway rat. It does not come from Norway but that is where it was first seen.

A brown rat is not always brown. Some are grey. Black rats are not completely black.

These pet rats are all kinds of brown rat.

hooded rat

golden rat

spotted rat

white rat

Water rats are
not rats at all.
They are voles. water vole

But people try to kill wild rats if
they see them. So brown rats live in
places where people do not often go,
places with plenty of water.

SEWERS!

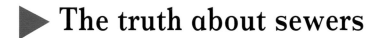 The truth about sewers

Sewers are underground pipes that carry away waste water. Some of these pipes are a few centimetres across. In big cities they can be several metres across.

Sewers have to be inspected, but there are not many people walking about down there. The rats feel safe in a sewer. They would not live there if they did not have to hide from people.

And who built the sewers?

Not the rats.

Did you know...

There are two kinds of sewers. Storm drains carry away rain water. The other kind carry water from kitchens, bathrooms and lavatories. Sometimes all the water runs into the same sewer. Water mains are underground pipes that carry clean water.

Disease and fleas

Rats do carry diseases but in this country very few people die because of rats. People carry diseases too.

We catch most diseases from each other, not from rats.

There is a dangerous disease called bubonic plague. People and rats can catch it, but people do not get plague from rat bites. A rat is sick. A flea bites the rat. Then that flea bites a person. Then the person is sick too. Even the flea is sick.

flea

Travelling rats

Remember, in Great Britain we live on islands. Rats first came to this country on ships. They brought the plague with them.

These days they are quite likely to travel by air. If someone sees a rat on an airliner the flight is delayed until the rat is caught.

Did you know...
All animals that have fur can have fleas. That is why they spend so much time scratching. Rats are furry.

▶ Teeth and tails

In cartoons rats have huge top front
teeth.

It is true that you can always see a
rat's teeth, but they are the bottom
ones, not the top. They are not really
all that huge but they have to be big
and strong because rats are rodents.

Rodents are animals that gnaw their
food. Their front teeth do not have
roots, like ours. As they get worn
down by gnawing, they keep growing.

Rats will eat anything. That is another reason why people hate them – they eat all the things that humans eat. They can also gnaw through electric cables. They are a great nuisance, but they are not "stealing". They are not like burglars.

And those tails...

Rat tails are not bald and scaly. They are covered in hair, but the hair is so fine you can hardly see it.

Look at your own arm. It is covered in hair but the hair is hard to see. How would you like someone to call you bald and scaly?

Rats need their tails to balance with. A climbing black rat can wrap its tail around a branch to steady itself.

Did you know...
Rats take great care of their tails and spend ages cleaning them. They hold them in their hands and wash a little bit at a time.

▶ Savage?

If you attack a rat it will run away.
If it is cornered it will turn and fight.
Most animals will do this. Humans do.

How can a little rat fight an enormous
person? There is only one thing it can
do, it bites. It may jump up but it will
not leap at your throat.

An adult human is bigger than the
biggest rat. Even a human baby is
bigger than the biggest rat.

Did you know...
People talk about giant rats the size of cats and dogs. Even tame rats seldom live more than two years. It would be hard to grow to the size of a cat in that time.

Adult brown rats are no more than 23 cm long and the tail is 18 cm at most.

Rats fight and sometimes kill each other, like other animals, but rats that live with people as pets are usually gentle and friendly.

They are also intelligent. I will tell you about one special rat. This is a true story.

Alex's rat

He was a brown-and-white hooded
rat and his name was Ratty. He
lived in a glass tank, the kind you
keep fish in. Rats like to see what is
going on around them.

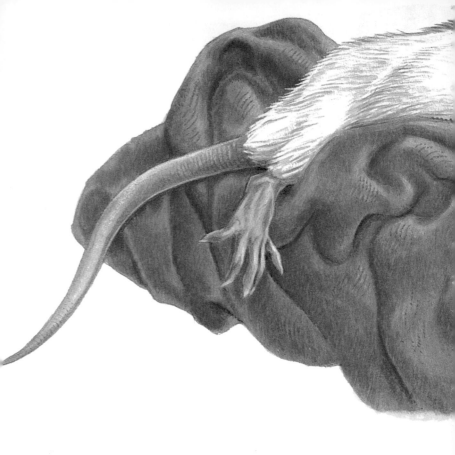

He had a brick to gnaw to keep his teeth trim, plenty to eat and plenty to drink.

He made a bed of shredded paper and sawdust every night, and every morning he cleared it away, pushing it aside with his hands.

One day Ratty was ill. He had
a pain, his pink hands and feet
went white.

Alex wrapped an old towel around a
hot water-bottle and laid him on it.
When Ratty felt better he went back
to his tank.

Next day when Alex put food in the tank, Ratty caught his sleeve in his teeth. He had never done that before. He did it again the next day. When Alex picked him up Ratty pulled at his shirt with his hands. Then Alex understood. Ratty was remembering the towel. He did not want to sleep on sawdust any more. He wanted bedclothes.

Alex's mum did not have time to
make little rat sheets, but every day
she gave Ratty clean tissues. Every
night he made himself a bed with
tissue sheets and every morning he
cleared it away.

I was Alex's mum. Even though we
could not talk to one another Ratty
could tell us what he wanted.

▶ Rats v people

People will go on killing wild rats because they are vermin.

Vermin are animals that live where people do not want them to live. This does not mean that the animals are dirty or wicked.

Did you know...
Weeds are plants that grow where people do not want them to, like dandelions and nettles. Usually, weeds are very successful, too.

And people hate rats because they are successful. This means that they do not go away and they do not die out. Whatever you do, there are always more rats.

People think that there are too many rats.

Rats probably think that there are too many people.

▶ Glossary

 burrows Burrows are tunnels dug in the earth by animals that live or sleep underground.

10

 disease A disease is an illness.

4, 14

 fleas Fleas are insects that suck blood.

14, 15

 gnaw To gnaw means to bite with the front teeth. The back teeth are for chewing and grinding.

16, 17, 24

 primates Primates are the animals most like humans, such as monkeys, gorillas and chimpanzees.

7

savage Savage means wild *and* fierce. Not all wild animals are fierce. **5, 21**

 scaly Scaly means covered in scales. These are plates of horn or bone that cover the skins of animals like fishes and snakes. **5, 18**

 water voles A water vole is a rodent but it is much smaller than a rat and eats only plants. **11**

OXFORD

WILD READS

WILD READS will help your child develop a love of reading and
a lasting curiosity about our world. See the websites and places
to visit below to learn more about rats.

Rats

WEBSITES

http://www.bristolzoo.org.uk/learning/animals/mammals/mole-rat

PLACES TO VISIT

Whether as pets or pests, rats have lived alongside humans for thousands of years.
Some people keep rats as pets and you may be able to see them in
pet shops. Otherwise you might spot one running from under a
rubbish bin or out of a drain!